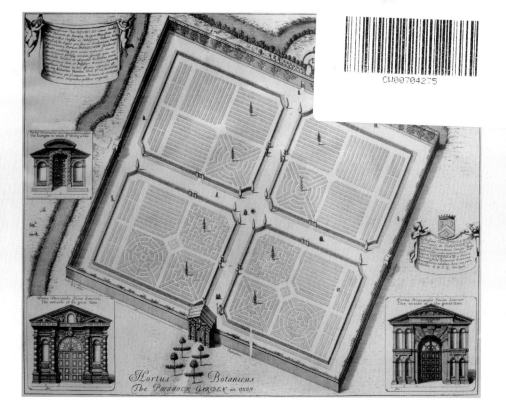

Hortus Botanicus
The PHISICK GARDEN in OXON

A LITTLE
SOUVENIR

The University of Oxford Botanic Garden and Harcourt Arboretum

Jill and Timothy Walker

Thistles in the sunset
2   Harcourt Arboretum, Meadow

Introduction

The Botanic Garden, originally known as the Physic Garden, was founded in 1621 by Henry Danvers, Earl of Danby, in order to provide the plants needed for teaching medicine at Oxford. The Garden was extremely formal with plants laid out in long narrow beds in order that the students could gather round the beds whilst the Professor lectured. Entrance was limited to the fortunate few and each quarter was surrounded by yew hedges and locked gates. However, the Physic Garden proved to be a jewel in the crown of the University. Visiting dignitaries were often brought to the Garden to be shown its rarities.

Thistle at Sunset in Harcourt Arboretum

Today the Garden is still a highlight of any visit to Oxford but one that is available to anyone. The yew hedges and locked gates are gone. The long narrow beds still exist in the Walled Garden demonstrating the different plant families but now the Garden extends into the Lower Garden with a stunning Herbaceous Border, Water Garden and Wild Flower Borders, not to mention the Vegetable Beds. For those with a taste for the exotic the Glasshouses on the bank of the River Cherwell provide plants from arid environments to humid rainforests.

Everlasting sweet pea (*Lathyrus tingitanus* 'Roseus')
Botanic Garden, Walled Garden

In just one visit you can journey in your imagination from one country to another, savoring the diversity that is the plant kingdom.

And if this is not enough, a visit to the Harcourt Arboretum, six miles south of the Garden, will extend your plant adventures even further. The Arboretum was acquired by the Garden in 1963 and provides the perfect antithesis to the formality of the Garden. A serpentine walk, banked with rhododendrons, snakes around a collection of mature and semi-mature trees from all over the world. In May the floor of the oak woodland is a carpet of intense azure blue as the bluebells emerge. From June the meadows are awash with a yellow haze of buttercups and hum with insect life. In Autumn the Acer Glade is a feast of fiery reds, oranges and yellows.

Any day of the year there is something to surprise, beguile and delight the visitor.

Autumn in the Acer Glade
Harcourt Arboretum, Acer Glade

Nepenthes
Botanic Garden, Lily House

Cytisus battandieri
Botanic Garden, Lower Garden

Autumnal acer leaf
Harcourt Arboretum, Acer Glade

Spring light
Harcourt Arboretum, Birch Woodland and Coppice

Lobster claw (*Heliconia pendula*)
Botanic Garden, Palm House

Witch hazel (*Hamamelis x intermedia*)
Harcourt Arboretum, Acer Glade

Parasol mushroom (*Macrolepiota procera*)
Harcourt Arboretum, Acer Glade

Larch cone (*Laryx decidua*)
Harcourt Arboretum, Acer Glade

Chinese yellow banana (*Musa lasiocarpa*)
Botanic Garden, Glasshouse Corridor

Autumnal oak (*Quercus robur*) and larch (*Laryx decidua*)
16   Harcourt Arboretum, Acer Glade

Daylily (*Hemerocallis* sp.)
Botanic Garden, Water Garden

Passion flower (*Passiflora quadrangularis*)
Botanic Garden, Lily House

Pollen-laden anthers of the Californian tree poppy (*Romneya coulteri*)
Botanic Garden, Family Beds

Herbaceous Border in summer
Botanic Garden

Sunflowers (*Helianthus* cv.)
Botanic Garden, Family Beds

Yellow skunk cabbage (*Lysichiton americanus*)
Botanic Garden, Water Garden

Japanese anemone (*Anemone* x *hybrida* 'Honorine Jobert')
Botanic Garden, Walnut Bed

Californian poppy (*Escholzia californica*) and Chocolate Joe Pye weed (*Eupatorium rugosum* 'Chocolate')

Botanic Garden, Autumn Border

Papyrus (*Cyperus papyrus*)
Botanic Garden, Lily House

Witch hazel in the snow (*Hamamelis mollis*)
Botanic Garden, Walled Garden

McCabe rhododendron (*Rhododendron macabeanum*)
Harcourt Arboretum, Serpentine Ride

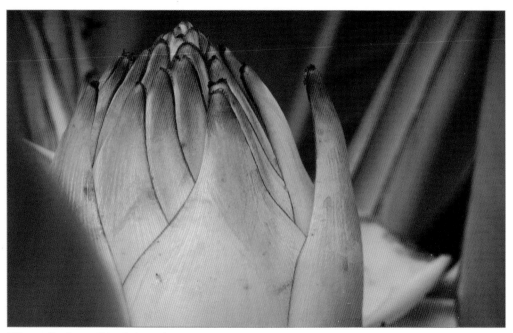

Chinese yellow banana (*Musa lasiocarpa*)
Botanic Garden, Glasshouse Corridor

Bracken understory
Harcourt Arboretum, Acer Glade

Daubeny's waterlily (*Nymphaea* x *daubenyana*)
Botanic Garden, Lily House

The Herbaceous Border in summer
Botanic Garden

Southern entrance into the Lower Garden

Botanic Garden

The Danby Arch and Family Beds
Botanic Garden

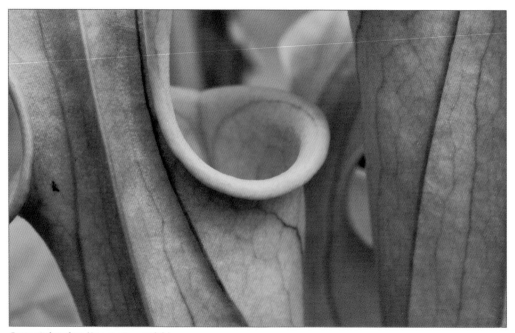

Green pitcher plant (*Sarracenia oreophila*)
36 Botanic Garden, Insectivorous House

Yellow latan palm (*Latania verschaffeltii*)
Botanic Garden, Palm House

Lyra's bench
Botanic Garden, Water Garden

View from the black pine (*Pinus nigra*) to Magdalen College Tower
Botanic Garden

Two views of a cold, crisp morning in the Botanic Garden

Botanic Garden, Lower Garden

Dittany (*Dictamnus albus* var. *purpureus*) and Magdalen Tower
Botanic Garden

The Danby Arch and the Fountain Pond
Botanic Garden

Jade vine (*Strongylodon macrobotrys*)
44 Botanic Garden, Lily House

Puya (*Puya alpestris*)
Botanic Garden, Conservatory

English bluebells at the Arboretum
Harcourt Arboretum, Bluebell Wood 47

English bluebell flowers (*Hyacinthoides non-scripta*)
Harcourt Arboretum, Bluebell Wood

Spring crocuses (*Crocus tommasinianus* 'Whitewell Purple')
Botanic Garden, Walled Garden

Pincushion flower (*Scabiosa lachnophylla*)
Botanic Garden, Merton Borders

Santa Cruz waterlily (*Victoria cruziana*)
Botanic Garden, Lily House

The fantastically smelly dragon arum (*Dracunculus vulgaris*)
52 Botanic Garden, Conservatory

Emerging flower of papyrus (*Cyperus papyrus*)
Botanic Garden, Lily House

Dewdrops on the stamens of an aster (*Aster* 'Little Carlow')
Botanic Garden, Autumn Border

The extraordinary flowers of the blue passionflower (*Passiflora caerulea*)
54 Botanic Garden, Family Beds

Foxglove tree (*Paulownia tomentosa*)
Botanic Garden, Lower Garden

Castlemilk Moorit sheep grazing at Harcourt Arboretum

Herbaceous border

Botanic Garden

Glasshouses and River Cherwell
Botanic Garden

Spring-flowering Yulan magnolia (*Magnolia denudata*)
Botanic Garden, Danby Arch

Icy sea holly flowers (*Eryngium planum* 'Blaukappe')
Botanic Garden, Merton Borders

Purple coneflower (*Echinacea purpurea*)
Botanic Garden, Merton Borders

Voluptuous flowers of the Spanish dagger (*Yucca gloriosa* 'Tricolor')
Botanic Garden, Family Beds

The OXFORD BOTANIC GARDEN and HARCOURT ARBORETUM are primarily a resource for teaching and research for the University of Oxford but learning about the plant kingdom and nature in general is not limited to the University. It is available to everybody. If every individual learns just one new fact during their visit, the Garden and Arboretum are fulfilling their purpose. But in reality the Garden and Arboretum are more than just a teaching resource. They are a source of inspiration to gardeners, writers and artists, a place of retreat and peace for individuals and a place of fun and adventure for the family.

First published 2014 for The Oxford Botanic Garden, contact: 01865 286690
www.harcourt-arboretum.ox.ac.uk and **www.botanic-garden.ox.ac.uk**
Photos by Jill and Timothy Walker, with additions from Chris Andrews. All material © The Oxford Botanic Garden. **ISBN 978 1909759022**
All rights reserved. No part of this publication may be reproduced, stored in a retrieval system, or transmitted, in any form or by any means, without prior permission of the copyright holder. The right of the Oxford Botanic Garden as the author of this work has been asserted in accordance with the Copyright, Designs and Patents Act 1988

Front Cover: **Foxgloves and the Danby Arch**

Title Page: **Herbaceous Border**

Back cover: **Spring crocuses**

Produced by
Chris Andrews Publications Ltd,
Oxford.
01865 723404
www.cap-ox.com